I0352017

JESUS IS THE KING OF KINGS

JESUS IS THE MIRACLE WORKER

JESUS IS THE GREAT PHYSICIAN

JESUS IS THE SON OF GOD

JESUS IS THE ALPHA OMEGA

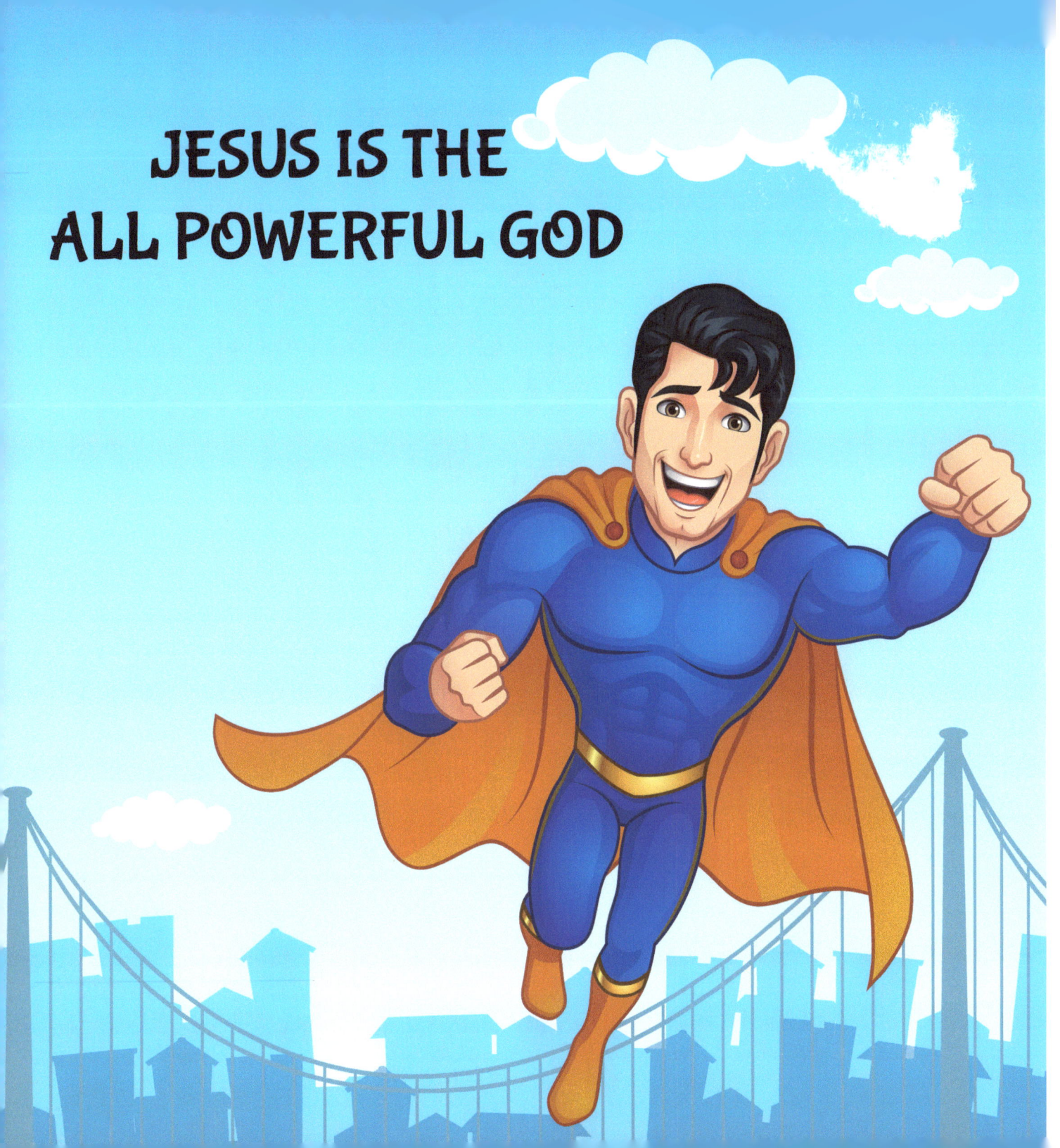

JESUS IS THE GREAT PROVIDER

JESUS IS THE GOOD SHEPHERD

JESUS IS THE MERCIFUL GOD

JESUS IS THE
BRIGHT AND MORNING STAR

JESUS IS THE LILY OF THE VALLEY

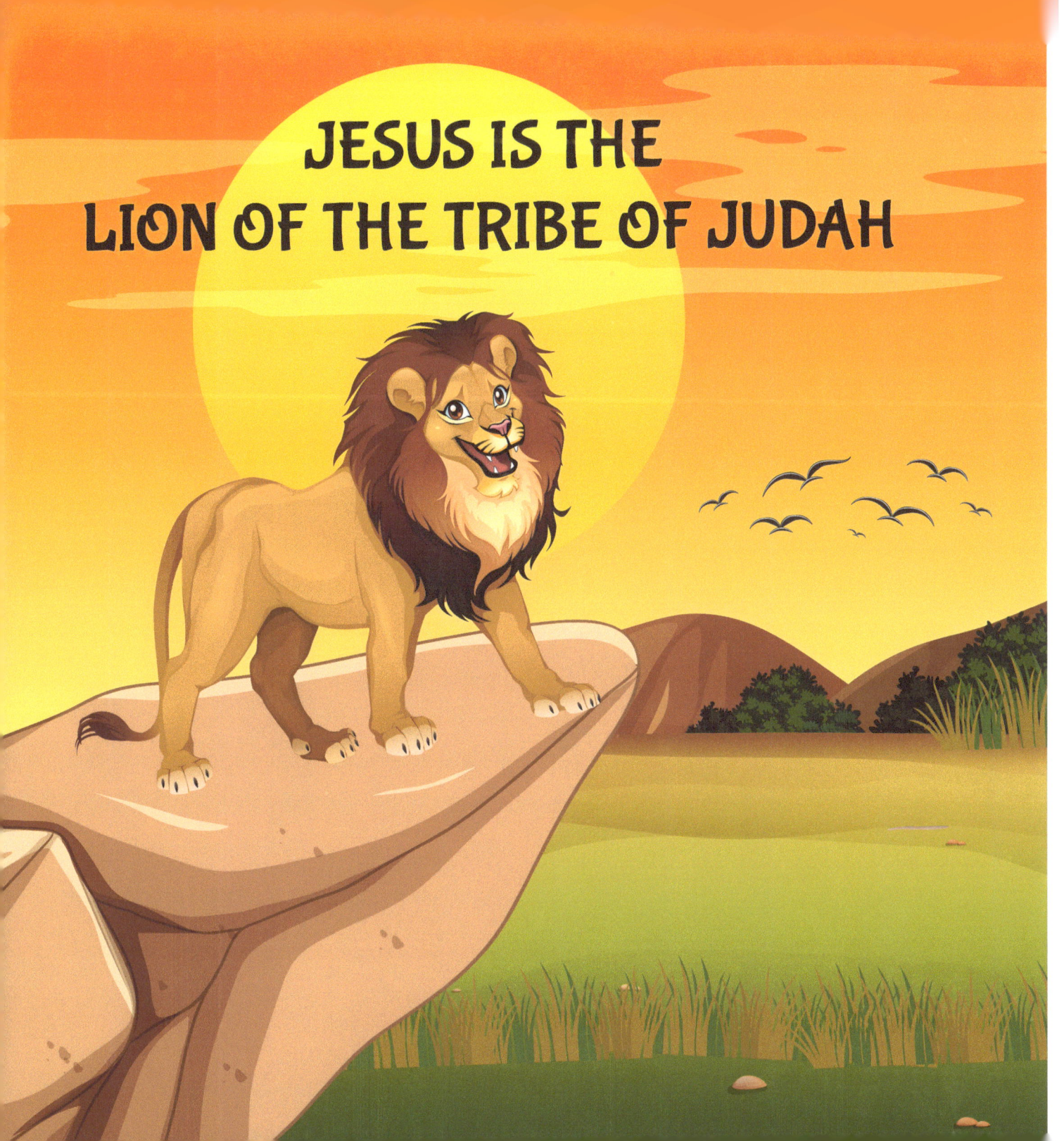

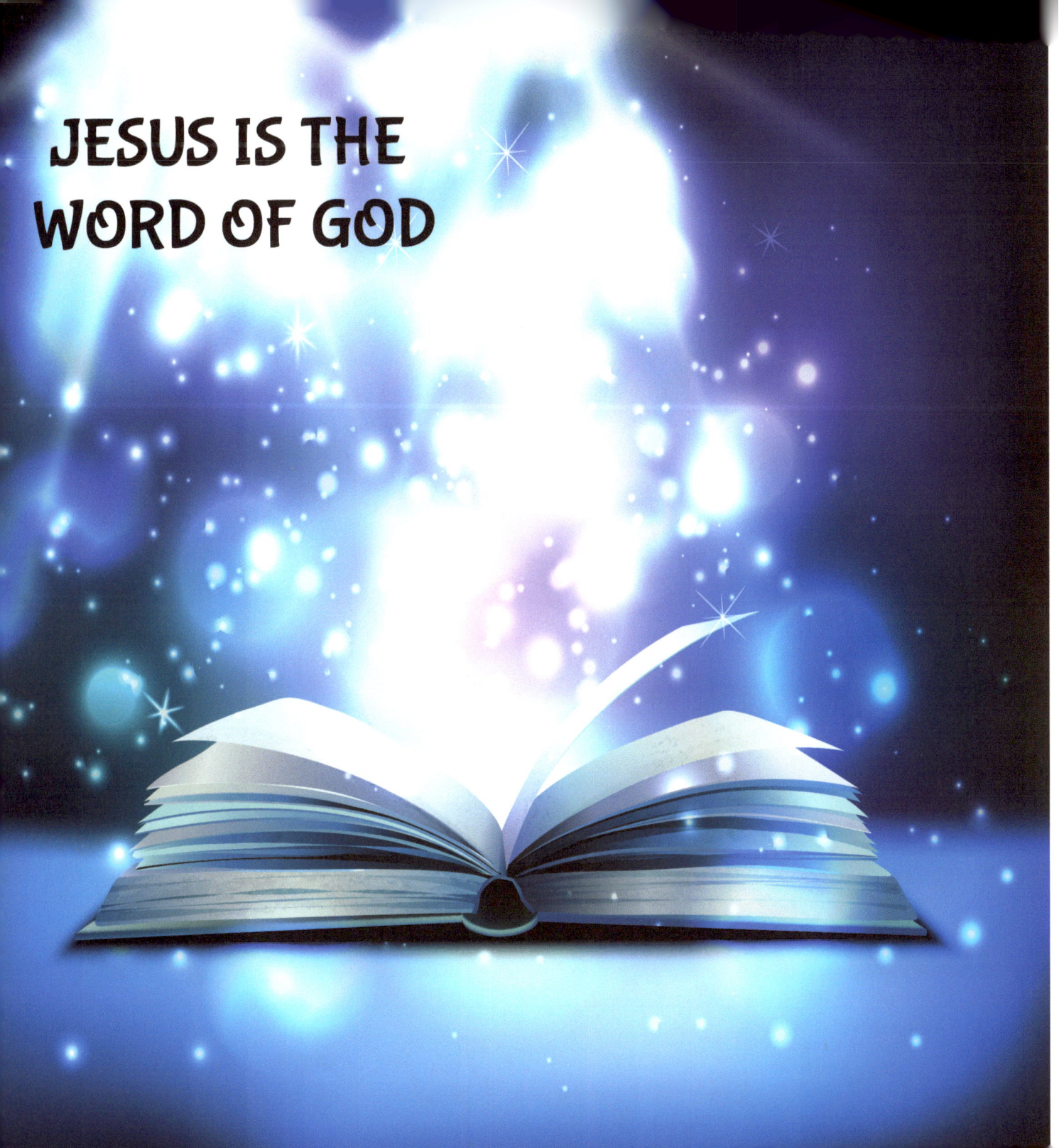

JESUS IS THE WORD OF GOD

JESUS IS THE DOOR

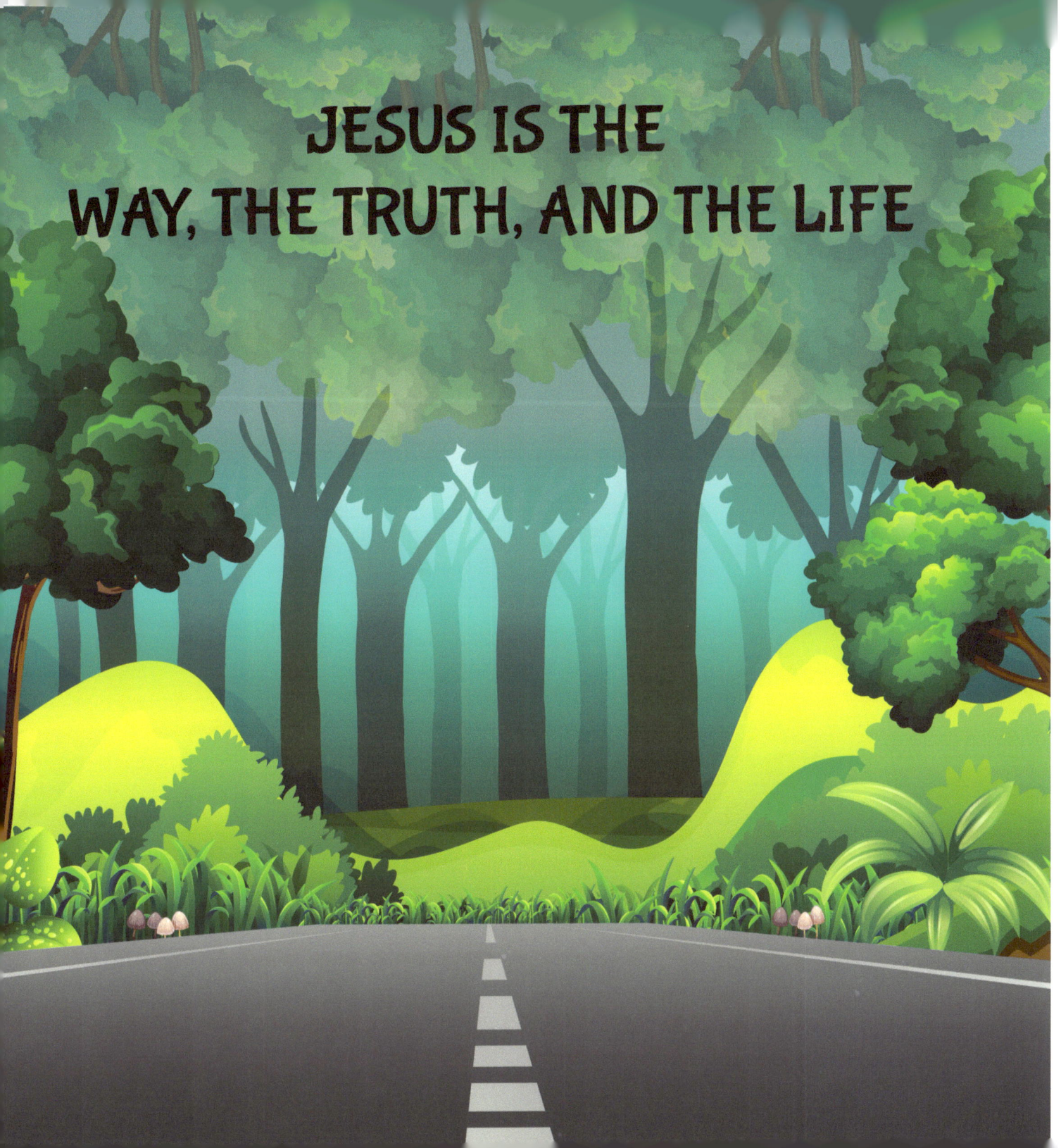

JESUS IS THE WISDOM OF GOD

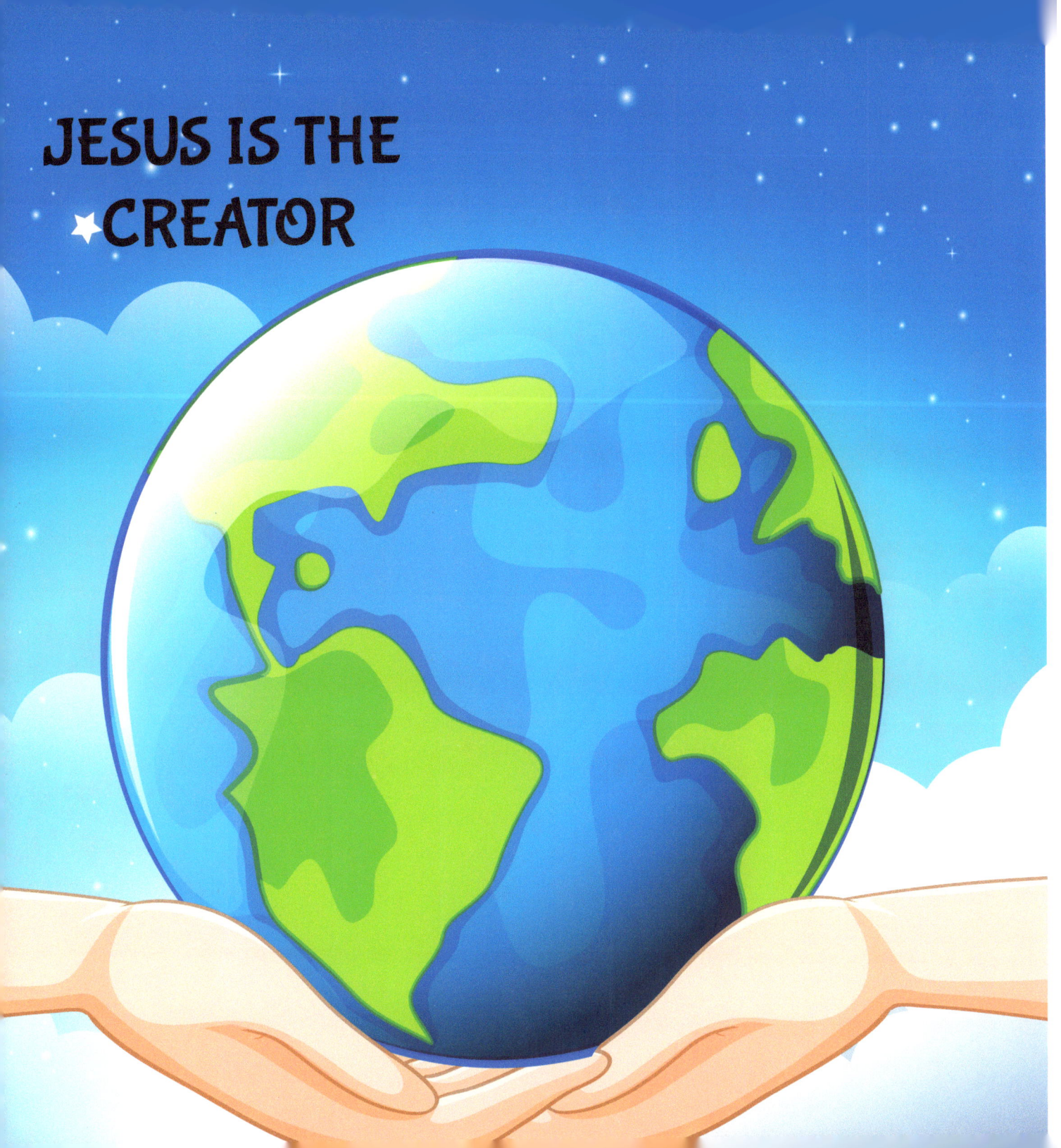

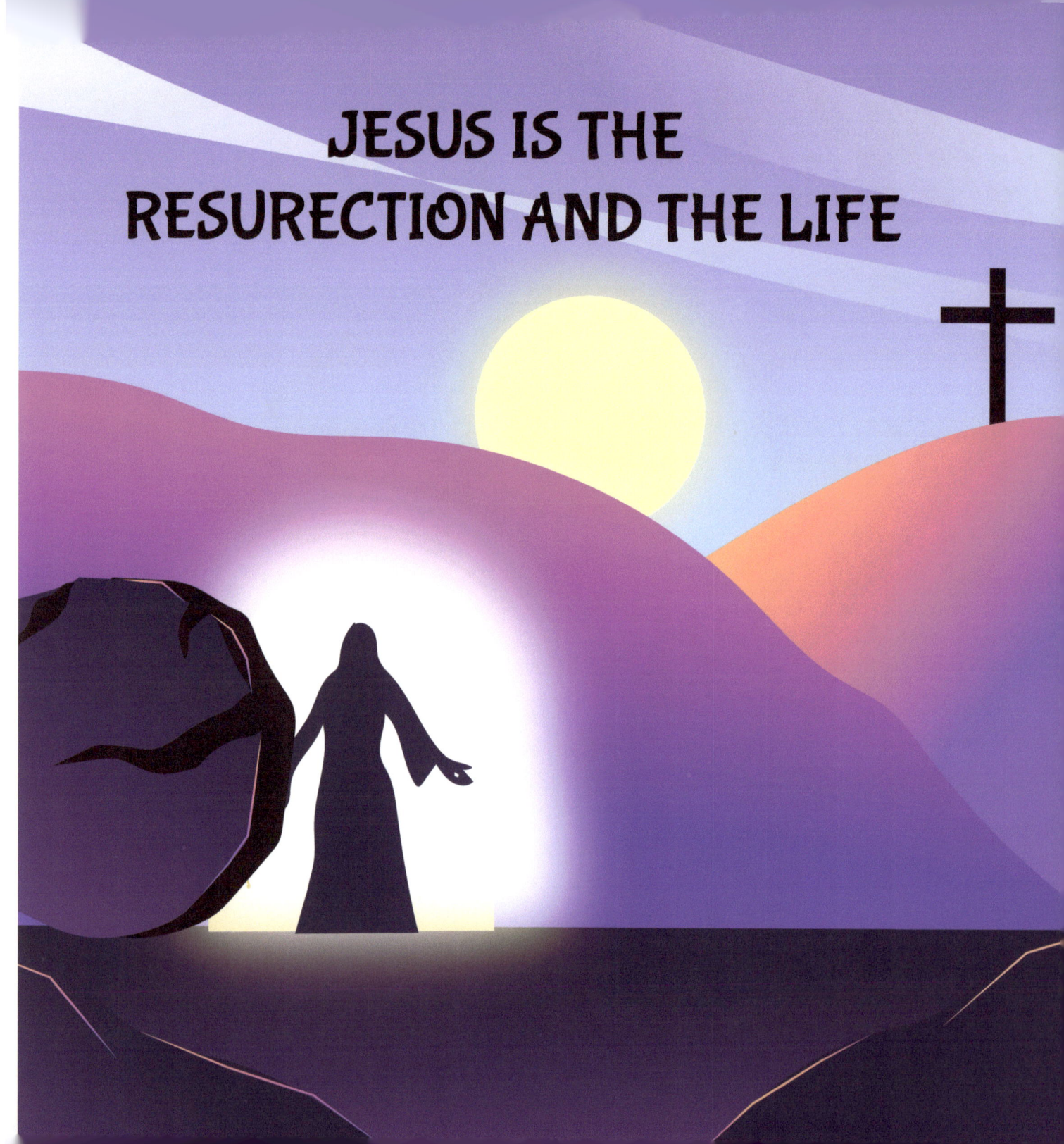

JESUS IS THE LIGHT OF THE WORLD

JESUS IS THE MIGHTY GOD

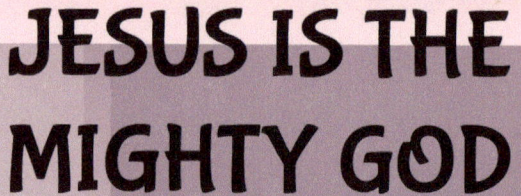

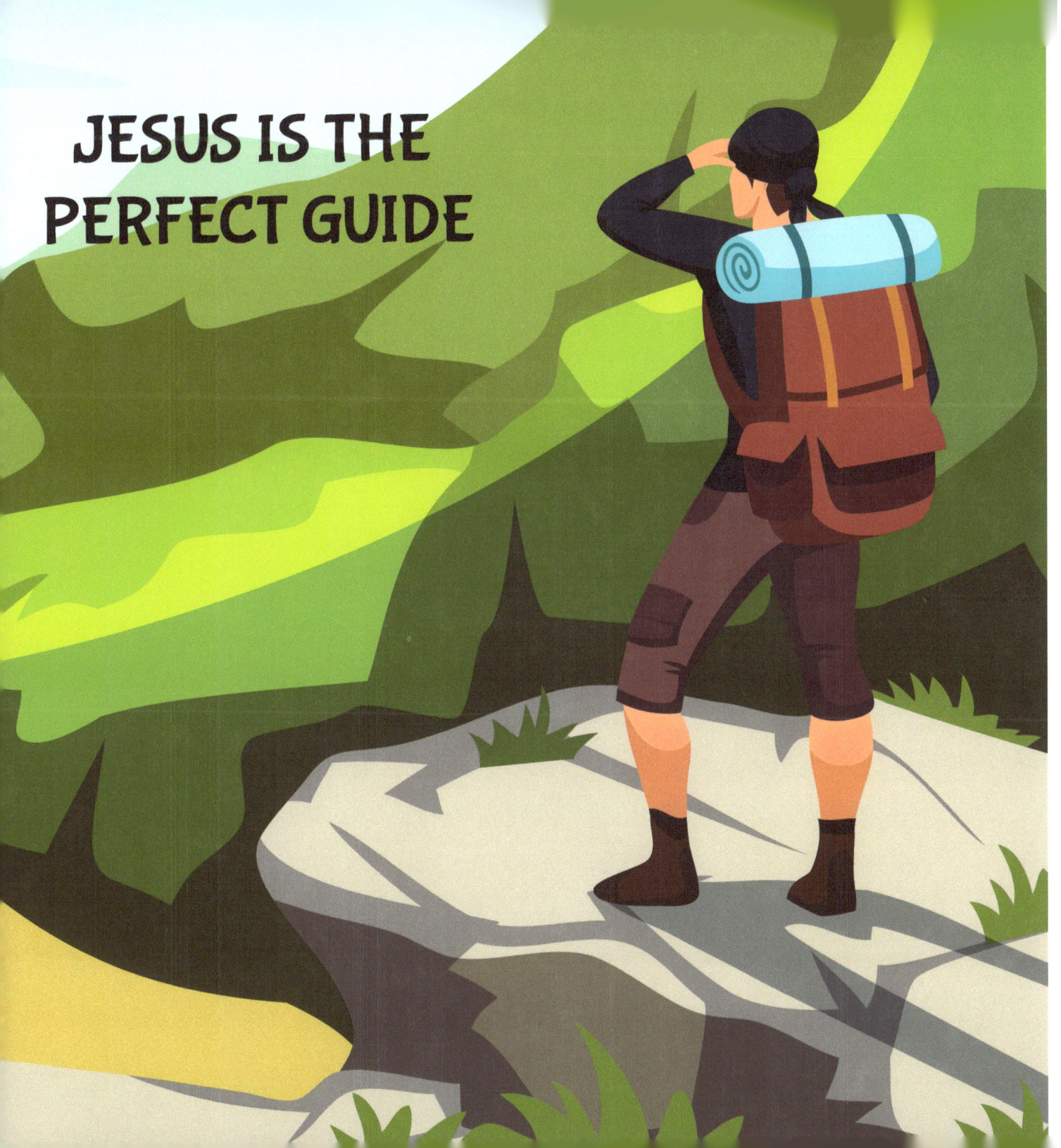

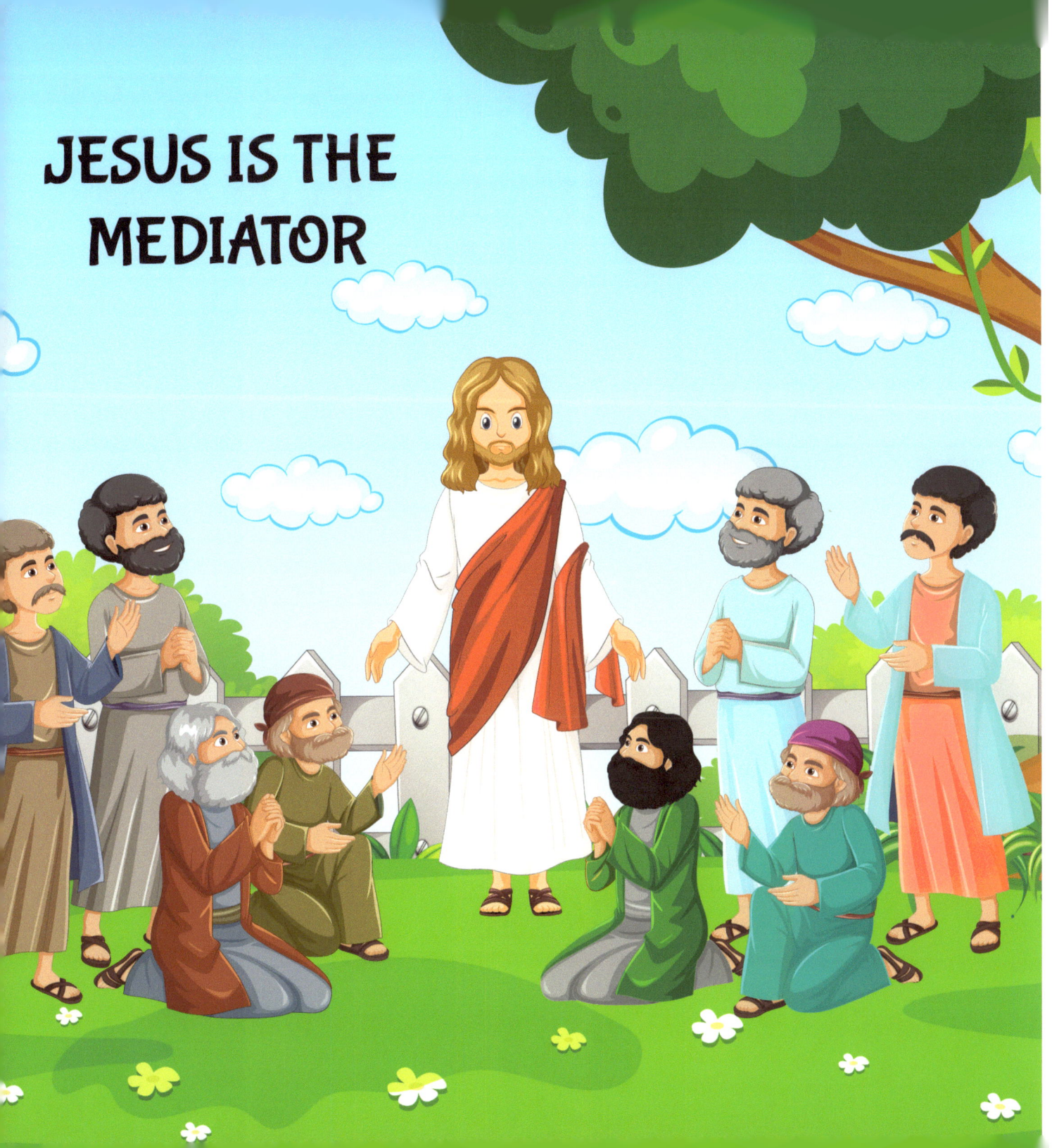

www.ingramcontent.com/pod-product-compliance
Lightning Source LLC
Chambersburg PA
CBHW041415010526
44107CB00016B/1176